EVERYDAY
FAITH
**LETTERS**
*for* CHRISTIANS

LETTERS *for* CHRISTIANS

# Tiekie PRESS

Letters for Christians series
Everyday Faith Letters for Christians

Copyright © Pieter de Kock, 2025
All rights reserved.

First published 2025 by Tiekie Press

ISBN 978-1-0686586-6-2

Edited and typeset by Copy-editing Services
https://copy-editing.org/

Cover design by Pieter de Kock

EVERYDAY FAITH

*for*

**Tizzy Simon**

*in memory of*

**Andrew**

They will still bear fruit in old age,
they will stay fresh and green,
proclaiming, "The Lord is upright;
he is my Rock, and there is no wickedness in him."
—Psalm 92:14–15 (NIV)

# LETTERS *for* CHRISTIANS

EVERYDAY FAITH

# FOREWORD

This foreword is written in our memory by a special friend who's no longer with us. Once a band of brothers—incomplete together in every sense of the word—time had marched on and we now found ourselves at the edge of his bed. His house was open; so was his heart. We cracked jokes to take the edge off his terminal condition but he was out of time and we were running out of jokes. One of his best friends was running out of patience as we searched for more jokes instead of more prayer. To say we needed faith to get through this was an understatement. But our inspiration came from Andrew himself. Unable to speak, dehydrated and in pain, he was calm as he got to know more about you Lord. He watched us all but from his steady gaze there was no judgement. He'd found you Lord. For those of us who knew and understood Andrew it was an honour to see him bravely complete his race. He reached out to take our hands and we saw how he shone with courage and faith. THE LORD is powerful in everyday life. It was He who sent His servant to pray over Andrew at the end. And then Andrew was gone. But not forgotten—just fallen asleep in the Lord's hands before being finally reunited in God's kingdom.

LETTERS *for* CHRISTIANS

EVERYDAY FAITH

# PREFACE

This pocket book follows on from *Everyday Love* and *Everyday Incomplete* in the *Letters for Christians* series. The first two were intended for readers of all ages and every level of Christian maturity but *Everyday Faith* is, in parts, unapologetically serious because, apart from love, if there's one thing we must have, it's faith. It's a spiritual necessity. The minds of children are being attacked as never before through technology and artificial intelligence and so we must sing about THE LORD's deeds and what HE has done before it's too late for them. This contains 92 letters with the 92nd being Psalm 92. It's we who write to THE LORD because HE'S OUR FATHER and we're HIS children. We should be encouraged to write our own letters to THE LORD. It's exercise for the mind and will strengthen our faith that way. Each letter ends with a short prayer to set the mind for when it's time for us to pick our own Bible up and explore the full context of GOD's word.

*Blessings*
*—may the Lord be with us all.*

*Amen*

LETTERS *for* CHRISTIANS

EVERYDAY FAITH

# INTRODUCTION

Every day we must have faith. We can't hope to remain connected to GOD without faith. It's a controversial subject because we all think we have it. Until it's time to be put to the test. And with every test we may find at some point we're not as strong as we once thought. Talk is cheap and THE LORD is not fooled. Perhaps we'll find where we stand more easily by reading Psalm 92 again. It's a psalm for the day of rest—when we make time to concentrate our thoughts on what GOD'S new covenant means for us all. HE'S defeated our enemies at the cross. HE is our rock now as HE was then. HE'LL protect us now as HE protected us then. We'll bear fruit in our old age now just as we did then. HE'LL do all these things if we praise HIM now as we praised HIM then. Hallelujah!

*Lord, you alone are upright, you are our rock, and there is no wickedness in you.*

*Amen*

EVERYDAY FAITH

# 1
# FAITH

Faith is a word like love: easy to mischaracterize. It can be applied in many ways. For example, we can be told by friends to get out of a certain place because it's become unbearable but for faith, people's advice doesn't matter. It's when GOD speaks, as in the case of Lot, that it matters. It's not faith to follow someone over a cliff or jump into a fire. Faith is pure. It's purity is in the action to trust, not anyone, but to trust GOD. We become faithful by being the least among men, ready to serve, always forgiving and spiritually uplifting. It's only when we humble ourselves that we're able to have faith.

*Lord, may we have true faith—to do what you tell us to do.*

*Amen*

LETTERS *for* CHRISTIANS

## 2
## SHIELD

Faith in the Bible isn't a helmet, sword, belt, or breastplate. It could have been any of those but it's described as a shield. It's something we use to defend ourselves from attack and we use it on our weaker arm with the sword of the Spirit in our leading hand. So, we push back in faith and strike our enemy using the word of GOD. None of this is through our own strength but our power is from THE LORD. Our shield represents HIS mercy and forgiveness as we defend ourselves against the flaming arrows of the evil one; rejecting the accusations that are hurled at us from the powers of darkness.

*Thank you Lord, for our shield against the evil one.*

*Amen*

EVERYDAY FAITH

## 3
# WHO STAYED

While many of us now form part of a brave diaspora, very few have had the faith to remain behind in trying circumstances. For every ten of us who were brave enough to leave, one of us was brave enough to stay. Those that have remained with their faith intact will be greatly rewarded because it's not an easy thing to do. Abandoned, threatened, persecuted, lives turned upside down by an unrepentant enemy—and yet onwards they've struggled. May THE LORD bless them, their children, and for those that have gone, may THE LORD bless their memory.

*Thank you Lord, for those who remained behind, their faith intact.*

*Amen*

LETTERS *for* CHRISTIANS

# 4
# FULL OF FAITH

A dog is faithful but it has no faith. It's not full of faith. We can be faithful and full of faith but it's better to be full of faith. To be faithful is a passive condition—it needs someone to instruct us; while being full of faith is an active state—we're ready and watchful, constantly reconciling what we see with what we hear from THE LORD.

*Lord, help us to be full of faith.*

*Amen*

EVERYDAY FAITH

## 5
# CUT OFF

If one of the greatest acts of faith was Abraham's willingness to sacrifice his son Isaac, the jury is out about some of the biggest acts of unbelief. Our experience with mobile phones must rank highly though. How many of us experience a panic attack when we've left home without it? How uncomfortable we've been while away, the whole time unable to constantly check whether we've checked it. Yet, less than 35 years ago we had no idea what a mobile phone was. Today we're driven by fear, acting as if we're incapacitated and lost but we don't seem to have that same angst about our relationship with GOD. Our reliance on the phone is a sign of weakness because the devil has convinced us that we've been cut off. Fortunately we don't need a mobile phone for GOD. HE'S always there in our hearts and we never have to worry about leaving HIM behind.

*Lord, help us rid ourselves of gadgets that track us and make us feel insecure.*

*Amen*

LETTERS *for* CHRISTIANS

## 6
## SHARING

The privatisation of public services such as railways, hospitals, schools, universities, airways, water, postal services, power, and other infrastructure is almost always a massive disappointment. The promise never matches what's been given up in collective ownership, despite the flashy branding and subtle brainwashing. We're told to have faith as performance is compromised and profits soaked up elsewhere. When the world tells us to have faith we know it's an empty promise but when GOD tells us to have faith we're transformed because in GOD's kingdom we share in what's produced: joy.

*Thank you Lord, that we can share the fruits of our faith in you.*

*Amen*

EVERYDAY FAITH

## 7
# QUALITY CONTROL

In this world we have to have faith that the things we're eating aren't harmful to us. The same goes for the things we use, that they're properly made. But often they aren't. Just take a look at some of the ingredients in processed food or shortcuts taken by manufacturers. The same goes for our health services. It becomes all too clear that where there's money to be made the first thing that suffers is quality, which is why we depend on strict regulation for protection. GOD doesn't protect us in the same way. All HE'S looking for is sincere repentance. When we're born again HE doesn't need strict regulations to control our behaviour because through HIS mercy and grace we're rich beyond measure so there's no need for us to compromise on quality.

*Thank you Lord, that we don't need to make money in your kingdom because we're rich beyond measure.*

*Amen*

LETTERS *for* CHRISTIANS

## 8
# PICK UP

If we'd bought a ticket to fly somewhere and someone said they'd pick us up at the airport, we'd have faith that they would. But if they said they'd pick us up at the airport in a hot air balloon we'd lose our faith in them. For us to have faith we have to believe the entire message. Our faith in JESUS rests with HIS entire message. If we book our tickets, get on that plane, fly to HIM, HE'LL be there to pick us up when our journey of repentance is over. If the promise includes being whisked away in a hot air balloon with champagne corks popping, then the message is from the devil. We are literally picked up off the floor when we've repented and the reward is simply that we're safe in his hands. There's no need for any more fantasy from this world.

*Thank you Lord, for picking us up and getting us home.*

*Amen*

EVERYDAY FAITH

# 9
# DANCE OF FAITH

Faith has such power that we can't be condemned if we have faith in CHRIST. Perhaps that's what David had above all else, faith in GOD. That, for all his shortcomings and despite all his talent, it was how full of faith he was as he danced and sang unashamedly for GOD. Even when his wife despised him for it.

*Lord, may we have a smidgen of the faith that David had so we can dance for glory.*

*Amen*

LETTERS *for* CHRISTIANS

# 10
# SHIELD

That great shield: Faith!
   It allows us into a fight, protects us when we pray,
   while we spread the word, and even as we stray.
   And if one day we find ourselves without our shield to stay,
   unclothed we be, a pitiful sight, and very easy prey.
   There'd be no cover, no place to know, how we should now be,
   only that we must run away, as far as eye can see.

*Lord, may we never lose faith in you.*

*Amen*

EVERYDAY FAITH

# 11
# BRIGHT OR STORMY

We can't feel someone else's pain nor can they feel ours. The same is true for emotional distress. We've no way of experiencing what others are experiencing. As for faith, it can't be measured or quantified. Everyday faith is as ordinary as the light that comes in through our windows in the mornings. Just as our rooms are lit up, so too our relationships. We know people of faith by their fruit. If they always seem to light up a room chances are they're strong believers. But if the room is constantly blackened by dark storm clouds every day, then faith is missing. Like pain, we can't measure it but where there's no faith, there's no light.

*Lord, help us to seek the light because where there's light, there's faith.*

*Amen*

LETTERS *for* CHRISTIANS

# 12
# CHILDREN

When we're children we never stop to think about the dangers in what we get up to. Walking barefoot along sheer cliffs there's never a thought given to slipping and falling, or snakes, or wild animals. There isn't even a hint of fallibility as we scamper up vertical cracks in large overhanging rock formations. There are no barriers between us and instant death yet we creep up to the edges overlooking land hundred's of meters below. Children are special to THE LORD for a reason: the absence of fear and the presence of faith.

*Make us your children Lord, slow to fear and strong in faith.*

*Amen*

EVERYDAY FAITH

## 13
## COUGHS & COLDS

Coughs and colds are beyond irritating. They drag on for ages and have a habit of resurfacing without reason. There's no command or pill that will do away with them so we generally try to ignore them and get on with things. The same thing can be said for many types of sin. We don't engage yet we're engaged by them; a niggle constantly taunting us. Sometimes it's best to get on with what THE LORD wants us to do and, with that shift in mindset, the cold no longer matters and before we know it, is no longer in our lives.

*Lord, help us to know when to stop attending to distractions so that they no longer matter.*

*Amen*

LETTERS *for* CHRISTIANS

## 14
## BE STILL

A veterinary practice has a sign asking people to watch out for when the candles placed on their reception desk, are burning. This is to show respect for the owners of a deceased animal. It's a nice gesture and one can't think of any circumstances in which this request would be ignored. It's also a good strategy for a church to adopt for people who are struggling in their faith. There's no need for an announcement, just respect from one to another as people try to cope in difficult times—because sometimes we just want to be still.

*Lord, our best moments with you are when we are still.*

*Amen*

EVERYDAY FAITH

## 15
# BUMPETY BUMP

If we've ever kept bumping into the same person in different places and wondered what the reason could be, it's tempting to think we're being asked to intervene in their lives. But the only way to find this out is to get a conversation going. Sometimes the conversation seems meaningless and we think that the lesson to be learnt is in our lives, not theirs. But sometimes it's best to leave the lesson to be learnt in their lives. It's not always the case that we're required to say anything profound but just to be that person they keep on bumping into.

*Lord, our interactions are yours and may we never assume your interactions are ours.*

*Amen*

LETTERS *for* CHRISTIANS

## 16
# REVENGE

When mistakes are made in hospitals, difficult procedures such as performing a tricky operation can in a sense be forgiven. But when the mistakes are as simple as going into a patient's room and wanting to administer a cocktail of drugs that would cause serious damage or death, it's almost unforgivable. Forgiveness of this kind requires massive amounts of faith. There are many situations we find ourselves in everyday life, when every part of our being wants to take revenge but, for followers of CHRIST, we can never go there or be that person.

*Lord, one the biggest lessons from your New Covenant is that revenge is yours, not ours.*

*Amen*

EVERYDAY FAITH

# 17
## SCOPES

The devil is like an assassin, roaming this earth in search of souls to destroy. But to be able to take people out he needs to be able to see us clearly in his scopes. Being desperate, weak, lonely, or unworthy doesn't allow him to focus in on us; it's only when we're full of pride, like he is, that he's able to *really* focus in on us.

*Lord, help us to understand what the enemy is looking for when he tries to destroy us and take steps to avoid them.*

*Amen*

LETTERS *for* CHRISTIANS

## 18
# PSEUDO FAITH

Having faith to build a house when you have millions in a bank account isn't that impressive. Having faith to build when you have no money is much more impressive (or foolish). The same goes for acts of faith. David fronting up to Goliath was truly inspirational but if he'd attacked with many soldiers fully kitted out, it would have been less impressive as an act of faith. We're all building houses in God's kingdom and some are exceptional. It's the ones we build that seem doomed to fail which are the best when they succeed.

*Lord, help us to have more real faith and less pseudo faith.*

*Amen*

EVERYDAY FAITH

# 19
## REALITIES

It's quite scary to think of the possibility that everything we thought we knew about life, isn't true. The everyday in life's services, entertainment, regulations, court rulings, traditions, right down to the stack of invoices on our desk, are the things we've enacted. They're constructs we've brought to bear. In another reality every single person we've known may not be who we think they are, which begs the question: do we know who *we* are? But the faith we have in GOD is the only reality we need to be concerned with. Our favourite road along the beachfront past the roadhouse is really just something fleeting and meaningless in another reality. But whatever the truth is (or was) in our lives, it's our faith that assures us of the eternal truth of JESUS CHRIST OUR SAVIOUR. Which things we recognise in heaven is anyone's guess but it probably won't include that roadhouse.

*Lord, let's not wonder about the reality of heaven and just be full of wonder at your reality here on earth.*

*Amen*

LETTERS *for* CHRISTIANS

## 20
## TERMINAL

The news comes in. It's the same news from someone else a few years ago. "I have terminal cancer" a dear friend says. The finality of it doesn't yet sink in so we make a few jokes, "I might beat you" someone says. "Can I borrow your BMW" someone else quips. But we're never prepared because it's hard to imagine that we're going to die. "At least you know and can get ready, make plans" someone else says. Plans? There can only be one plan: salvation in the body of CHRIST. When we die we live. There can be no greater everyday faith than facing death but the devil has a habit of keeping us busy, distracted, sometimes with an unhealthy level of humour and bravado. But faith conquers them all and love keeps us together

*Thank you Lord: when we die, we live!*

*Amen*

EVERYDAY FAITH

## 21
## OURS TO LOSE

We may often have marvelled at what some people have in this world, even as we acknowledge the role played by their perseverance and hard work. THE LORD blesses those in HIS flock who have much; but HE blesses those who have little, more. When we have little we're able to see more clearly through the fog of the spiritual war raging in front of us every day. We notice things that others might miss. Our search for wisdom is rewarded many times over without having to worry about where all our cash is, our property portfolio and invested shares. Those who have much deserve extra care because what they stand to lose exceeds the disappointment of those who have less—many times over.

*Lord, we pray for those who have much in this world, that they don't lose sight of the cross.*

*Amen*

LETTERS *for* CHRISTIANS

## 22
## HIS IMAGE

Fractals are tiny repeating things, like the leaves on a tree. They provide visual stimulation which we as humans can't really do without. The best way to understand them is by lying on our back looking up at a tree's canopy. It's full of fractal-like elements. We could watch for hours. It's maybe the reason why we can't take our eyes off a fireplace as the flames constantly layer meaning upon meaning in mesmerising combinations. Now if we were sat in front of a blank plastered wall our analogies would turn to hell. It's the human condition—we're not good with things that have no detail or interest. We don't do alienation well. GOD made us in a special way because we're made in HIS image, which means that whatever HIS image represents, it's full of wonder, beauty, and richness—the likes of which we've yet to see.

*Praise God!—that we're able to share in what has been prepared for us. What a day that will be!*

*Amen*

EVERYDAY FAITH

## 23
## SUB-ZERO

Going out in sub-zero temperatures with the flu isn't a pleasant experience. But we often have to and so we do. The air feels like it's about to tear our throat away. The next day it feels worse and our head's pounding, our nose constantly dripping. The third day we have to stop for breath every now and again. But one thing we know is that flu doesn't last forever and at some point the burning sensation starts receding until we've forgotten what flu feels like. We're good at forgetting bad experiences. And yet we're not so good at forgetting sin. Our sins have been forgiven and forgotten at the cross so why do they appear before us like the flu, taunting and incomplete? It's because it's *we* who can't forget. But THE LORD has—so when the accuser is around, it's up to us to raise that shield of faith and stand firm.

*Lord, help us to overcome the great manipulator of this world.*

*Amen*

LETTERS *for* CHRISTIANS

# 24
# ALL OK?

One of the biggest complaints people have about religion is that it makes them feel worthless and guilty. They're so fed up they've decided it's a process that can't be trusted. Because "we're really not guilty of anything!" we hear them say. Jesus warned us that whoever forgives little, loves little. It's equally true that whoever finds little reason to repent is unable to repent properly. The idea that we're all ok and don't need to go down on our knees to beg for forgiveness, is to be deceived and misled. It's also arrogant and a very dangerous place to be in.

*Lord, lead us away from arrogant self-love, towards the love that Christ has for us.*

*Amen*

EVERYDAY FAITH

## 25
## BLIND

Faith is often compared to being blind and without faith, we are. But while we may try to understand what it's like to be blind by closing our eyes, blind people can't open theirs to see what it's like not to be. And it's true for us spiritually because even as HIS children, we can't open our eyes to see what GOD sees because the time hasn't come. And until then, with faith that amounts to less than a mustard seed, we're almost completely blind.

*Lord, we're almost completely blind but you are our rock.*

*Amen*

LETTERS *for* CHRISTIANS

## 26
## SELFIE TRAIL

Our vanity is surpassed only by our own ego. And while we may try our best to trivialise the crippling effect, it's part of the family of pride. Don't we sometimes feel self congratulatory or superior only to stifle those feelings and then not do away with them in a righteous manner? Facebook, especially, started to own us in this way as we crafted stories and images of ourselves and then laboured away to speak truth to what we'd created. Our phones then provided the ideal tool for perpetuating the lie. Nowadays it's seldom possible to tell a Christian apart in a crowd, because their mobile phones are always out, pointed at themselves. But if there's one thing others should notice immediately about followers of CHRIST, it's that we're not followers of ourselves.

*Lord, keep us from being preoccupied with ourselves so that we can become preoccupied with you.*

*Amen*

EVERYDAY FAITH

## 27
## IMPOSTER

There's a reason we're all so reliant on what other people think. It's because the devil knows what the most tempting thought in our mind is. It's that we've no need for GOD; we *are* god. It's been the same message since the Garden of Eden. It's the devil's message. So when we squirm or feel embarrassed as others belittle our creator and test our faith, our reaction is to feel like an imposter. The trouble is, it's the reaction which puts us in most danger and if what others think is more important to us than GOD, then we're lost.

*Lord, your ways are not our ways and there's no other way but your way.*

*Amen*

LETTERS *for* CHRISTIANS

# 28
# IMPRESSIONS

It's much more liberating to not have to impress anyone—because then we're free. When we need to impress people there's a huge amount that comes into play because to impress requires us to be boastful in some way. Sometimes we might even find ourselves being boastful about how humble we are. In other words, we often end up lying. The most common reply we'll hear about being oneself is from people who say, "Well, that's how we are all the time, we've got nothing to hide." But sadly it's not true. We always have to take care to impress others in some way. We just wouldn't survive long if we all walked around being ourselves. So, it's fair to say that it depends on *who* we're trying to impress. If we're trying to impress GOD then we're careful around people, in what we say and do because, fairly or unfairly, they'll form an impression of GOD from how impressed they are with us.

*Thank you Lord that we can boast of your work in our lives.*

*Amen*

EVERYDAY FAITH

# 29
# TO BOAST

Many of the words used in the Bible weren't meant in the same way we mean them today. *Hate* is one. *Boast* is another and is one of those words that has negative connotations. It's a 'shouty' kind of word. It feels arrogant and insincere—and yet it's used in a positive way in the New Testament to boast about OUR LORD JESUS CHRIST. But perhaps the best summary of the use of this word can be found in the Old Testament:

This is what the Lord says:
"Let not the wise boast of their wisdom
 or the strong boast of their strength
 or the rich boast of their riches,
 but let the one who boasts boast about this:
 that they have the understanding to know me,
 that I am the Lord, who exercises kindness,
 justice and righteousness on earth,
 for in these I delight,"
declares the Lord.
                    Jeremiah 9: 23-24 (NIV)

*Lord, let our boast be in faith about you.*

*Amen*

LETTERS *for* CHRISTIANS

# 30
# WALK THE WALK

Everyday faith represents our walk with GOD. If we're a bit shaky it'll show. If we like walking ahead, it'll really show. If we like sitting rather than walking, we won't be going very far. But if we walk with purpose—thinking, watching, praying—our walks will be the most meaningful of all that we do. Every day.

*Every day Lord, help us to walk the walk.*

*Amen*

EVERYDAY FAITH

# 31
# THE CLOSEST TREE

If ever we want to look for signs of weakness in our personal relationship with THE LORD we need a keen eye. Somewhere along the line we may have felt hairline cracks in our temperament or behaviour which we've dismissed at first. But if we've ever noticed cracking under a pathway the first thing to do is look for the nearest tree. Tree roots can travel and can cause damage under pathways and buildings, which aren't noticeable for years until it's too late and quite expensive to repair. In our lives tree roots can mean anything which starts getting in the way of normal everyday faith. All we need do is to just take a look around us. We'll spot the problem soon enough.

*Lord, help us to look out for signs of weakness in our faith so that we can fix whatever the problem is early.*

*Amen*

LETTERS *for* CHRISTIANS

## 32
# DIFFERENT PATHS

Everyday faith for every one of us means following different pathways. The biggest mistake we can make is to watch someone else or try to mimic them because we'll become confused. It's true for when someone else stumbles as it is for when we ourselves stumble. We're different so we can't all be walking the exact same path. And because we're different, we shouldn't compare what we've gone through with what we think anyone else is going through.

*Help us to stop comparing Lord, because just as your disciples were all different, so are we.*

*Amen*

## 33
## LOVE

When asked who loves us the most we'll automatically point to our mother. A mother's love may be strong but it's only as strong as the human mind. GOD's love for us is so powerful we don't comprehend it. We try to understand love through the cross but our minds are too weak to process the totality of that love. But it doesn't matter because the little we are able to process about what we mean to HIM, is enough to sustain us in faith.

*Lord, thank you for your love even if we are limited in our understanding of the breadth, and length, and depth, and height of it.*

*Amen*

LETTERS *for* CHRISTIANS

# 34
# STORM

It's easier finding our way along a path during or after a storm partly because the water shows us where to go. After a downpour all the animal tracks are a lot more visible and reflecting pools of water help us with direction. On a sunny day the same terrain would look very different. Faith is a bit like that. When things aren't going well we're in stormy conditions and everything in front of us has been washed away. But it's opened up all the pathways for us more clearly. On the other hand, when things are going well with us and it's nice and sunny, we tend to think we don't need our faith as much because we can see everything. Except for those pathways which the storm would have revealed which are now hidden from us.

*Lord, help us to understand how what appear to be ideal conditions don't necessarily mean we're in ideal conditions.*

*Amen*

EVERYDAY FAITH

## 35
## WHO ARE YOU?

How do we find out more about ourselves? Prayer is a good start. Another sure-fire way is to open our mouths and see what comes out. We're mostly disappointed though because we're able to say some pretty stupid things. What we say as well as what we don't say reflects who we are. But not saying something can also be pretty stupid sometimes. So, unless we're told to be quiet, giving an opinion is the way to go because it teaches us about ourselves and helps us grow as Christians. Often the more wrong we are, the more we're able to grow. THE LORD wants us up and about, thinking, trying to understand what our role might be in changing circumstances so that, when HE needs us to act, we're able to act wisely.

*Make us confident in your ways Lord, so that we know when to speak and when to be quiet.*

*Amen*

LETTERS *for* CHRISTIANS

## 36
# NOT PERFECT?

People have been known to commit suicide because the image they wanted to present to this world wasn't perfect enough. One of our biggest mistakes we can make is to make our own self worth conditional on the image we present in public. To be seen to be struggling is for many, an admission of failure; of not having been saved properly. Nothing could be further from the truth. The late David Pawson described how his troubles only started after he was born again and if someone were to accuse him of sin he'd say it wasn't even the half of it. You see, it's the devil's most piercing accusations: "Thought you'd be perfect? Haven't you stopped sinning?" It catches a few of us out because we want to be just perfect! When we're burdened in this way it's time to turn in the Bible to your forgiveness at the cross and let it all sink in again, then raise that shield of faith against the evil one.

*Lord, we've been saved but we're not perfect. You are!*

*Amen*

EVERYDAY FAITH

## 37
## KEEPING FAITH

Some people think faith is being able to trust that the sun will rise tomorrow. Others think of faith in terms of the toaster working or the car starting. It's not certain the car will start until it's been started. Faith also happens depending on how we respond when things don't happen as we expect them to. No toast: mild irritation but faith intact; car not starting: mild panic but faith intact. And if the sun doesn't rise on a foggy morning we don't lose faith because we know the darkness has given way to a new day; it's just that we can't see the sun. But if the tree outside is brighter the sun must have risen. If we can't see what we're hoping to see our faith tells us to look at something else. As Christians we can spin into a mild panic and think "Where are you Lord?"—but it's as easy as looking at where and what HE wants us to see because THE HOLY SPIRIT always points us in the right direction.

*Lord, help us to have faith and to trust you even when you don't appear to be next to us.*

*Amen*

LETTERS *for* CHRISTIANS

## 38
# BLUE DUIKER

There are small antelope called blue duiker which are extremely difficult to observe during the day. But with enough patience we can get to know these beautiful little creatures. Ever wondered why we were meant to see some things? Sometimes the only way GOD can get us to see what HE wants us to see is to stop us looking at what we want to look at. Every morning most of us want to see the sun in the sky. We don't like looking at dreary scenery. Some scenes however only exist when there's no sun. Blue duiker move around in deep shade. Our faith sometimes does too. It requires us to see places which we'd normally avoid because how else is GOD able to show us different things when all we want to do is stand in the sun.

*Lord, your wisdom is beyond human comprehension. Help us to get out the sun and stand in the shade for a while.*

*Amen*

EVERYDAY FAITH

## 39
## COLD INSIDE

One of the mistakes we can make if we need to be active in cold weather is to put too many layers of clothing on. It's when perspiration from our skin can't dry out quickly enough that we become cold on the inside no matter how warmly dressed we are. Our faith in CHRIST can sometimes be affected by having too many protective layers between ourselves and people around us. It's good to insulate ourselves from the world but when we become a little colder on the inside, that's when to stop. Because life isn't meant to be lived cut off from people; only from their sin. Our dislike shouldn't be of people, but of their behaviour. What we wear then should only have enough layers to ward off the effects of bad behaviour on us.

*Help us to dress properly Lord, so that we're never cold on the inside.*

*Amen*

LETTERS *for* CHRISTIANS

## 40
## STANDBY

More and more people have a standby generator just in case the mains power goes off. It can last a while but only until its source of power runs out. We have batteries for some things but only for as long as they can hold a charge. After that we're stuck with candles which last as long as their wax. Then at the most basic level we're back to sitting around a fire doing what needs to be done. It doesn't take much imagination to realise the importance of that fire for our basic needs but for our spiritual energy we're born again and that energy never runs out.

*Thank you Lord, for a source of energy that never runs out: You.*

*Amen*

EVERYDAY FAITH

# 41
# REST

When tossing and turning to get to sleep, who hasn't tried solving the problem by counting sheep; only to find it doesn't work because there's one sheep that can't jump the fence. Then we think of the number twelve. The twelve disciples. That'll work, we think. But there were only eleven after Judas. Twelve months in a year, twelve seconds; twelve times five equals sixty; which equals a minute. Eventually we're so exhausted that we simply get up and go and make a cup of tea. Rest is so important for us but so too is a clear mind. When we add too much to our lives it can feel a bit like not being able to get to sleep; and we start inventing new problems. Instead of creating problems we should try thinking about what we're grateful for. It's good to praise THE LORD in that way because that's when we de-clutter our minds—and before we know it, we're fast asleep!

*Thank you Lord, that when we focus on praising you we can clear our minds and be refreshed.*

*Amen*

LETTERS *for* CHRISTIANS

## 42
# BUILDINGS

Buildings are considered by many to be important to our experience of faith. They can be small chapels or large cathedrals but it's not so much the size that's important but the space itself. We're asked to contemplate the greatness of GOD in the intimacy and exquisite detailing of a chapel or in the booming reverberation under a cathedral's soaring roof. It's hard not to feel closer to GOD but we should be reminded that our faith has little to do with the building and everything to do with those gathered in them.

*Lord, fellowship with you is our building —always magnificent, always beautiful.*

*Amen*

EVERYDAY FAITH

# 43
# ENTRANCE DOOR

The entrance door to a house is easily the most important feature to be able to distinguish. We want everyone to know where we expect them to come in. But sometimes the front door is only symbolic and we want people to enter through the back or kitchen door. The give-away is a well trodden path. Church buildings tend to always use the main symbolic entrance but sometimes also a side door. The give-away in Christian faith is also a well worn path. It's easy to spot and it's where we want to be—because it's the path used by all the followers of CHRIST when they're born again and THE LORD can't wait to let us in.

*Thank you Lord, for the door to your house because the closer we get, the easier it is to recognise.*

*Amen*

LETTERS *for* CHRISTIANS

# 44
# BUNNIES AND BUNTING

Some houses have their Christmas decorations up well after the 6th of January which is the generally accepted date for them to be taken down. It's not clear where this rule comes from but it has to do with when the three wise men appeared twelve days after Christmas. It's the same for Easter where we're running around the garden like bunnies looking for Easter eggs. There's nothing in the Bible about these traditions. Jesus refers only to prophetic scripture from the Old Testament and to his death but we seem to be more taken with feasting and opening presents than we are with sacrifice and suffering.

*Lord, if it's not in the Bible then we should be wary about many traditions that celebrate you.*

*Amen*

EVERYDAY FAITH

## 45
## COOKIES

We all have different ways of saying goodbye to loved ones. Many final thoughts are deep and personal but on one headstone was written a recipe for cookies. If you've seen this and tried the recipe you'll know how delicious they are. One can't help feeling that this person was blessed in their lives because of the lightness of touch in that departing message.

*Lord, bless those with full hearts and draw them towards you, we pray.*

*Amen*

LETTERS *for* CHRISTIANS

# 46
# BELIEVERS STREET

Depending on where we live, our main streets or high streets are made up of the things that make the most money out of us. And in some urban areas this means betting shops, fast foods, nail shops, and convenience stores. Basically the things that cater to our craving for highly processed things and events. In some sense our vanity has also become a highly processed and toxic commodity. It's now highly refined, sickly sweet, and instantly applied. If faith were a high street it's tempting to think about what that would look like. Perhaps we can get a glimpse by imagining rows of shops owned by the early apostles because they'd be invested in making the most of us.

*Lord, help us to be people who make the most of others.*

*Amen*

EVERYDAY FAITH

## 47
## SAT NAV

We just know when our Sat Nav is taking us in the wrong direction even though it's very convincing. It happens frequently especially when we know there's a quicker, shorter route. The devil is like that, always wanting us on the longest route away from home as possible.

*Lord, help us to be aware of where you are so that we don't need to listen to any other voice.*

*Amen*

LETTERS *for* CHRISTIANS

# 48
# ENVIRONMENT

New countries are exciting until we realise that people are mostly the same wherever we go, even if the accent is different. But there is something that can have an effect on people and that's their environment. If we're in an oppressive environment whether it be by rule, class, or religious intolerance then we're often different in public. Our change in behaviour is an act of self preservation. Christians are asked to live by faith and not to be afraid but that doesn't mean we should be foolish either. Respect, but not afraid.

*Lord, help us to live righteous lives no matter where we live.*

*Amen*

EVERYDAY FAITH

## 49
## BELONGING

Were birds made for trees or trees made for birds? Both. If we follow the outline of a tree we come across branches that are birds—and they appear as if part of the tree. Then again, a tree belongs to birds: every twig, branch and trunk. But it's quite different with us because we're made for GOD; not, as some people think, that GOD is made for us.

*Lord, we're made for you, we belong to you, and creation is your gift to us.*

*Amen*

LETTERS *for* CHRISTIANS

# 50
# YESTERDAY'S HITS

Modern technology can have its benefits. Anyone who's looked up a song from their past, to play, or has wanted to check on the lyrics again can confirm how enjoyable it is to go back in time. But it's never just one song. Before we know it, three hours later, we're still belting them out and tapping a hole in the floor. What's interesting are the comments section which typically declare each song the best ever followed immediately by the inevitable moan about why things aren't as innocent today as they were in those days. It's an interesting phenomenon, the way we bend our perception of things, because were those days really as innocent as we make them out to be; and are the days we're living in now really as dark as we make them out to be? The answer really depends on our own spiritual health and levels of awareness.

*Lord, being spiritually healthy means we're switched on to your mercy but switched off to the dark matter.*

*Amen*

EVERYDAY FAITH

## 51
# GRAFFITI

The things that attract the most graffiti are symbols of power, either of something else, or ownership over us. We react negatively to signs in this world that imply ownership over us. It repulses us. There's something in us that defends our inalienable rights. In its essence, graffiti represents our collective reaction against being dominated by someone, some thing, or some system. It's a blunt instrument to be sure even if it bears a message that says no to being dominated. But in the KINGDOM OF GOD there's no need for graffiti because our inalienable rights remain intact, lovingly restored by JESUS and eternally reinforced by THE HOLY SPIRIT.

*Thank you Lord, for restoring us and keeping us renewed through your everlasting mercy.*

*Amen*

LETTERS *for* CHRISTIANS

# 52
# INSTRUCTIONS

In the old days an architect had to push their pencil around a piece of paper taped down to a flat drawing board. Nowadays they push light pixels around a flat screen to achieve the same outcome: a set of instructions. The set of instructions Moses returned with was carved in stone. Which set of instructions do we think has the greatest effect: paper thin symbols, a mixture of red, green, and blue light values; or heavy with words that one's fingers can recognise? What if the set of instructions couldn't be seen, only felt. Is it possible to forget an instruction which has been written into our hearts? No, it's impossible to forget those.

*Lord, it's impossible to pretend not to hear your instructions. Thank you.*

*Amen*

EVERYDAY FAITH

## 53
## OUR GOD

Each day of the week is named after some or other god, generally Nordic or Germanic; as are the months of the year. Life is a tapestry of superstition with meanings borrowed and swapped out in a complex web, spanning cultures and physical continents. It makes sense that we'll have invented reasons for our existence, created gods from what we saw around us or made with our own hands. And it was all too easy to subjugate others to gain power over them. THE GOD OF ISRAEL is different from every other god for two important reasons. Firstly, HE is holy and we may not make an image of HIM; and secondly, HE sent HIS SON to atone for our sins. We are forgiven. There is no unfinished business for us except that we shall forgive, just as HE forgave us.

*Lord, you are holy, we've been forgiven, and our own efforts are useless without your mercy.*

*Amen*

LETTERS *for* CHRISTIANS

## 54
## GOOD ENOUGH

When it comes to many of life's challenges we always seem to be up for the fight. Whether it's studying, building a career or family, playing sport, working on a hobby—we tackle them head on. But when it comes to our role as Christians so many of us completely fade away. We're not righteous enough, we say to ourselves. We're hypocrites we think quietly. Our thoughts are too conflicted, we pray earnestly. There's excuse after excuse and most of them are valid except for one thing: *when will we be good enough?* The answer in that state of mind is that we're never going to be good enough. It's a big problem because when we were born again THE LORD told us we were good enough—not because we are, but because HE paid the price and set us free. So, if what we do is not believe HIS promise then we've in fact denied HIM in front of everyone, just like Peter. Except worse.

*Lord, through your sacrifice you've told us we're good enough so there are no excuses from us.*

*Amen*

EVERYDAY FAITH

## 55
## FIGHT

For every group of people who've suffered and been in crisis, there have been many more who have enjoyed life with little regard for the welfare of others. And should any one of these suffer it's easy for those who've experienced it before to turn a cold shoulder. That's human nature: when we needed you, we were ignored and now it's pay back time. But that's not what we're taught as Christians. If we look at what's going on at a low level that's the way we're going to feel but if we understand the spiritual warfare going on then the human level is insignificant. It's our duty to step up wherever we can and fight for THE LORD.

*Lord, we know life isn't going to be easy because there are still so many who are like we once were: unrepentant.*

*Amen*

LETTERS *for* CHRISTIANS

# 56
# —INGS

For a while after we've stopped drinking, partying, socialising, and most other things ending with —*ing* such as lying, cheating, and deceiving it dawns on us how much time we have on our hands. Life is suddenly boring, we think to ourselves. We might sit around for a while thinking about backsliding but at some point we click. Filling our day with GOD'S work isn't for the faint-hearted. There's another kind of stamina needed. We need to be disciplined, to be thinking all the time, reading, and talking to THE LORD. The —*ings* here are laughing, praying, living, breathing, seeing, feeling. And then all of a sudden, we're sharing, caring, and connecting but this time it's a very different experience.

*Thank you Lord for when you help shift our minds from craving to joy.*

*Amen*

EVERYDAY FAITH

## 57
# EMPTY SHELL

There are things that are beautiful when they don't mean to be. They're especially beautiful if there's a sad story behind them. Take, for example, a half finished building in a semi-desert. There it stands—empty. It tells the tale of some person who ran out of money or the will to finish it off. But it's breathtakingly beautiful set against the flat, open surroundings and dwarfed by a huge soulless sky. There's nothing close by, not even a tree. It stands alone, windswept, cold, ignored, unclothed, incomplete. It moves us because it could have been our building. There are those who've begun their race after having been born again only to backslide and fall away and what's left is an empty shell, representing their efforts in holding on to GOD's promise. They said "Yes" but then denied HIM time and again, until what they meant was—"No." Still beautiful, but only a shell.

*Lord, may we always say what we mean and mean what we say.*

*Amen*

LETTERS *for* CHRISTIANS

## 58
## WALK!

Every day at the same time there would be a drumming sound coming from the corner of the room. It was the dog's tail announcing it was time to walk. Come rain or shine, that dog knew the time. It needed mental exercise that only the excitement of a walk could provide the animal. It's extraordinary how there are things in life we must all do to be content. For a dog it's to go on walks. For us it has to do with spiritual exercise. Without our conversation with THE LORD every day we risk triggering some form of mental decline. Not mental illness, but a decline in our levels of responsiveness as Christians. So, when we feel time creeping on and we're slightly on edge it's probably because it's time for our spiritual walk with THE LORD.

*Lord, let's not forget our spiritual walk with you every day.*

*Amen*

EVERYDAY FAITH

## 59
## POOR/RICH

The experience of having lived in one of the poorest countries in the world compares only to having lived in one of the richest. And the richest and poorest people can be found in both. It's not a mystery why either. The rich need the poor to remain poor; and in an odd way the poor need the rich just to stay alive. It's a relationship which doesn't work and will one day be done away with completely. Thank you LORD JESUS.

*Thank you Lord, for what we have to look forward to. Until then, you are with us.*

*Amen*

LETTERS *for* CHRISTIANS

## 60
# WEAK/STRONG

Many of us know the feeling of being without power. Not having money means we're weak and powerless in this world. But when we're weak GOD is strong. That's when GOD can take a situation and completely rearrange people's lives. Where there's weakness there's hope so we should be courageous especially when we're powerless because GOD is all-powerful.

*Lord, richly bless the weak and powerless of this world, for you are with them.*

*Amen*

EVERYDAY FAITH

## 61
## WE KNOW

Sometimes we have a feeling about someone or something which we later find out to be true. There are things in this world that are hard to define but we know it when we see it. Their meaning is inescapable. It's often called intuition or tacit knowledge, which is the human condition for knowledge which can't be expressed in words. THE HOLY SPIRIT provides us with all the understanding we need in this world to know when something is 'off'—even when we're not sure what it is we're looking at or why.

*If we stay close to you Lord, we'll understand even when we don't.*

*Amen*

LETTERS *for* CHRISTIANS

## 62
## HOPE

If faith is confidence in what we hope for and the assurance of what we don't see, is expecting to wake up tomorrow morning an act of faith? No, not if it's an expectation. If it's something we hope for then it is. We expect a lot of things from life, as if we're owed something. The strange thing is we don't often hear someone say they expect not to die, or they expect to be saved, go to heaven, or see JESUS. But we can have confidence in our hope that we'll be saved and we have assurance of JESUS who we don't see. The language we use tells as much about ourselves as our actions do. There are two parts to having confidence in what we don't see: it's to hope and to be assured.

*Lord, may we have hope and be assured, rather than an expectation, for what we don't see.*

*Amen*

EVERYDAY FAITH

## 63
## INCORRUPTIBLE

In the old days the images that were received by our brain were incorruptible. Everything out there was real. There were newspapers and magazines but our minds were able to process these without too much trouble. Then TV came along and after that videos, the internet, and an endless world of images through social media. Now with artificial intelligence we've been corrupted because our minds can't tell what's real and what's not. It's a good thing that our knowledge of GOD doesn't rely on images. Because if it did we'd corrupt our relationship with GOD too.

*Thank you Lord, that your presence is incorruptible in our minds, for you are the way and the truth and the life.*

*Amen*

LETTERS *for* CHRISTIANS

# 64
# CHANGES IN US

The images we see of ourselves from birth through the years are useful for understanding our physical journey. It's alarming too, for the sense of detachment we feel because, even if we accept ourselves in different states, it's difficult to reconcile how we thought of ourselves then with what we feel now. Our physical change is one thing but our spiritual journey can't be tracked. Only GOD knows what our spiritual journey looks like.

*Lord, let us hold on to our spiritual journey through life because that's the one that matters.*

*Amen*

EVERYDAY FAITH

## 65
# MOON

When looking at a full moon in the sky it's difficult to comprehend the reality of it. Barren and so far away—yet it stabilises the earth's rotation making life possible. So, something that has no life makes life possible hundreds of thousands of miles away. We're also psychologically impacted by it and it provides an endless source for the superstitious beliefs of mankind. But the moon is nothing more than a working part of GOD'S wonderful creation. Day or night it forms part of the physical framework providing what we need to live. But the reality of what we need to live isn't something like the moon, it's the *spiritual framework* we exist in: GOD'S forgiveness through JESUS CHRIST OUR LORD.

*Lord, may we never forget what allows us to live: the spiritual framework we call faith.*

*Amen*

LETTERS *for* CHRISTIANS

## 66
## AIM STRAIGHT

Darts is a game where we can achieve results by our own efforts, but it's not perfect. Aim for a triple 20 and we might get 1. Sometimes we're aiming for a 1 but we manage to hit the bullseye. It may be true for a while that the best players are able to get the scores they're looking for but they eventually make mistakes. In life we might be successful at what we do but when we throw a wrong one it can be GOD's way of reminding us that our own efforts are as superficial as a game of darts.

*Lord, thank you for reminding us to check our pride in at the entrance door to your kingdom.*

*Amen*

EVERYDAY FAITH

## 67
## READY

Someone once related how they went up a mountain for a leisurely hike and, three-quarters of the way up, one of the climbers collapsed and died. This was before mobile phones were carried around everywhere and he described the unpleasant experience of having to throw the body over his shoulder and take it down. It was quite an effort and had to be done in stages to save energy but also to make sure he himself didn't suffer a heart attack from the effort required. There are situations where we need to take care of ourselves first. It's just like putting that oxygen mask in a plane on first so that we can help others around us. Our spiritual health is important because in a crisis we need to be right with GOD to be able to make a difference around us.

*Lord, help us to keep spiritually fit, with our shield of faith at the ready.*

*Amen*

LETTERS *for* CHRISTIANS

## 68
# THREAT

Many families disintegrate towards the end especially when only one parent remains. The reason for this is normally greed and almost always triggered by someone who's married into the family. Sometimes it's caused by the siblings themselves. Either way it's a sad testament of a lack of character and faith. That respect that was once there disappears when the influence of a parent wanes. The family of OUR LORD JESUS CHRIST doesn't have the usual trigger points such as money and possessions but we do find situations where rivalry and jealousy become impediments to unity in our family. There's nothing to be done because money, possessions, rivalry, or jealousy have no place in GOD's church. To pursue this sinful behaviour is to condemn oneself.

*Lord, help us to withstand efforts by others to destroy once happy families.*

*Amen*

EVERYDAY FAITH

## 69
# BEWARE

"This book belongs to—" or " This whole room belongs to—." For those of us who went to boarding school every single thing we had was marked with our name on it and (if we had anything to do with it) an accompanying message like "Danger!" or "Beware!" Nowadays products have marks of ownership in the form of the ubiquitous barcode. It's the digital ID of products and services. And in the grand scheme of things we've also become a product so it won't be long before we need to have barcodes applied in some way. But then again we know this form of manipulation is coming because it's all in the book of Revelation. Our fingerprint will now be a machine readable barcode. This is offensive to GOD and we're reminded to resist this form of human bondage at all cost.

*Lord, let us be aware of being properly yoked for you alone are Lord and God.*

*Amen*

LETTERS *for* CHRISTIANS

## 70
## 2ND CHANCE

The desire to go back in time is a dream for some. But if we could, would we? And if we did, what would be the main reason? It seems like most people want to go back to say something to someone or just to hear their voice again. It's not so much to do something again but *to be someone again*. To be a bit kinder, more communicative, or more loving. To hug or hold someone. To sit and talk to someone again. To be more patient. To ask more questions. Sometimes we feel we could go back just so that we could try to be happier or less selfish, maybe less proud or vain. It's always about fixing a relationship or fixing ourselves. Mercifully we don't need to fantasise about this. CHRIST has fixed everything because HE'S seen the landscape we've inhabited—from when we were born right through to our final day. HE is all knowing and all seeing.

*We don't need a second chance or third chance Lord, because the first chance we got, we took—and were born again.*

*Amen*

EVERYDAY FAITH

## 71
# UNREQUITED HATE

There can't be a more poignant scene than watching old soldiers tell their story. For every one GOD-FEARING Christian there are scores of unrepentant souls determined to 'out-soldier' GOD. The fury in some—a sort of unrequited hate—is baffling and leaves a strong impression on us. The comments section inevitably follows the same theme, of a 'warrior' and 'legend'. "But what vanity is this?"—we think to ourselves; and we're reminded of Psalm 92: *for though the wicked spring up like grass ... they will be destroyed forever.* To depart this earth with such self admiration and boasting is foolish beyond words.

*Lord, may you reach into the obstinate hearts of those who wish to deny you to the bitter end; and save them from destruction, we pray.*

*Amen*

LETTERS *for* CHRISTIANS

## 72
# OUR FAULT

Life is not a long car journey where we have to sit in the back squashed up between siblings. In life we have all the room we need to move around. If we're feeling squashed up, it's our own fault. If we feel we don't have enough room to do the things we'd like to do, that's our own fault too. The only limiting thing in life is our own mind. GOD is right there and if we don't or can't see HIM, again, we're at fault. But GOD is patient and HE WILL wait until we're able to see the potential of life, HIS life.

*Thank you Lord, for your patience as we try to figure out what kind of life you'd like us to lead.*

*Amen*

EVERYDAY FAITH

## 73
## PLACES

We can leave a place but it never leaves us. We can go back to a place but it never returns to us. When we leave, the place goes with us: it's memories and it's people. When we go back, it's never the same; it never goes back with us. Our memories become floods of tears filled with imposters. It's an impossibility. There's no way around the finality of leaving or returning. But faith bridges the divide. Faith keeps us sane because we know the meaning of trust. Our trust is in GOD: *"I am the Alpha and the Omega," says the Lord God, "who is, and who was, and who is to come, the Almighty."*

*Thank you Lord, for being that one place which never changes.*

*Amen*

LETTERS *for* CHRISTIANS

## 74
## COMPLAINING

Who hasn't, in conversation with THE LORD, complained about their circumstances? It's a natural human thing to do but nine times out of ten, if we're listening, we realise how fortunate and blessed we are, where we are. We've been placed where HE wants us to be. We should be careful about complaining to THE LORD about our lot in life because if we complain enough, HE might listen and we probably won't like the results.

*Thank you Lord, for putting us where You want us to be.*

*Amen*

EVERYDAY FAITH

## 75
# DISRESPECTED

There are cases where people have experienced many years of mental abuse from the same person and every time the offender ignores the complaint, denies it, or accepts the accusation and simply says: "Forgive me,"—only to repeat the offensive behaviour with regularity. It's a tough one to deal with and tougher still because we're to forgive our brother or sister (fellow disciple) when they sin against us—and if they keep on sinning we're to keep on forgiving. The reason, JESUS explains, is because we've been forgiven at the cross. The burden has been lifted from us and justice lies in GOD's hands. It's unfinished business for GOD, not us. But if a brother or sister refuses to listen and repent, to even the church, then JESUS says we're to treat them like a pagan or tax collecter. Saying: "Forgive me" without true repentance, or refusing to stop the offensive behaviour, is to be disrespectful.

*Lord, may we have the patience to endure disrespectful behaviour and leave it over to you.*

*Amen*

LETTERS *for* CHRISTIANS

# 76
# ROADS

For most people there are always several roads to get home. Then there's our favourite road. We can close our eyes all the way but we'll know exactly where we are from the whine and revs of the engine, the tilt of the car, the way we speed up or slow down, and all the little bumps along the way. If the windows are down we know from the outside air and surrounding smells. Some of us have a favourite road through the Bible, others have favourite verses or pages where photos of loved ones and other special memories are stored. But the most favourite spiritual road we can be on is the road of faith and in our experiences from that journey.

*Lord, our favourite road is the one that leads straight towards you.*

*Amen*

EVERYDAY FAITH

## 77
## FIREPLACE

A fireplace has the capacity to completely rewire us. When there's a fire going we and the space we're in are transformed. It becomes our favourite space. When it's too warm for a fire it loses none of its attraction because it occupies the centre of our attention. The absent fire represents who we are and holds the entire room together. Faith is like a fireplace. Faith in action is a roaring fire which keeps and sustains us through the days when there's no fire going.

*Our hearts are like a roaring fire for you Lord, when it's cold outside; and even when it's not.*

*Amen*

LETTERS *for* CHRISTIANS

## 78
# BRIDGES

We have bridges over culverts, streams, rivers, ravines and gorges. Bridges connect us, they span hostile areas and provide links to new destinations. The Bible is a bridge between mankind and GOD—but only a few of us use it. THE HOLY SPIRIT is a spiritual bridge connecting the word of GOD with OUR REDEEMER—which only a few of us call on. And the cross is a bridge to GOD through our SAVIOUR—and only acknowledged by few. Surely THE LORD must sometimes wonder what the point was for building all these bridges—but HE never does. Such is HIS love for us.

*Thank you Lord, for building these bridges because there's no other way to reach you.*

*Amen*

EVERYDAY FAITH

## 79
## PALS

Everyone knows how valuable friends are but the most valuable are the one's we've grown up with and gone through life together, always staying in contact with one another. For some reason those people remained in our lives and it's a special thing—one worth celebrating. There are others who stopped being friends for a reason too. The reason doesn't really matter but a parallel can be drawn with how THE LORD knows who's left HIS side. But for those remaining faithful to the end the relationship is different because GOD isn't a friend. GOD is holy. Many of us who like to think of GOD as 'a buddy' may be in for a shock unless they reconsider their relationship in time.

*Lord God, you are Holy. Let us never forget that.*

*Amen*

LETTERS *for* CHRISTIANS

# 80
# POSSESSIONS

There are hoarders and there are people with an insatiable demand for cupboard space. The first will fill whatever space we give them with all kinds of stuff. The second does the same except is able to store them in an orderly way. Both are fixated on possessions. Hoarders are much maligned for good reason. Their dwelling becomes unhygienic and unliveable. Both have a problem letting go of things. One thing's certain, we can't take anything with us so why do some people desperately cling to things in this life? It has to with faith. Those with little faith need lots of possessions to fill a void in their lives while those with great faith don't need their possessions to control them.

*Lord, help us to let go of the unimportant things in life.*

*Amen*

EVERYDAY FAITH

## 81
## PANIC

It seems that as we get older we don't necessarily become wiser. We seem to become more susceptible to attack as we grapple with our own mortality. Some may call it existential angst but whatever it is, it threatens to derail us at some point. Some personality types love the idea of a last hurrah to rekindle some of that mischievousness from our youth. Other personality types stoke the flames of addiction. Just another drink, where's the harm, we say to ourselves. Then we have the adventurous bucket list types who plan trips all over the globe. We've not many years left, we think, so let's go out with a bang. The reality is we're all fooling ourselves. Not having many years left means we're closer than ever to GOD's wonderful promise which, if we have the faith to believe, should be all we need to focus on what HE wants from us before we go.

*Forgive us Lord, when we stumble because we should know what the antidote to panic is. It's faith.*

*Amen*

LETTERS *for* CHRISTIANS

## 82
## SKELETONS

Our body is the temple of THE HOLY SPIRIT and it's useful, in terms of our spiritual existence, to think about how we're made. For example, our skeleton is like THE WORD OF GOD. It's the structural frame and everything hangs off it. But to do something with that skeleton we need to be able to move—and for that we need faith. Faith is like the tendons and muscles that allow our skeleton to move and bend. It's the faith we need to do things which we can only get through the forgiveness of JESUS CHRIST. Then there's the oxygen which flows through our bodies bringing life to both skeleton and flesh. It's like GOD'S breath. It's THE HOLY SPIRIT speaking to us and inspiring others through us. So, in a way, the three main parts of our body together represent GOD'S WORD, JESUS CHRIST, and THE HOLY SPIRIT.

*Lord, we're beautifully made by you and we're encouraged by this.*

*Amen*

EVERYDAY FAITH

## 83
## LEAP OF FAITH

When a child needs a boost of confidence they've often been told to "take a leap of faith!" The message is to trust ourselves, try something new, and not to be scared. But Christians don't take leaps of faith. Where would we leap to, one wonders. We simply have faith. Faith is the result of action which produces more faith; and so we build ourselves up incrementally through consistently applying knowledge from GOD's word in conjunction with action from everyday experience.

*Lord, teach us the difference between leaping and doing.*

*Amen*

LETTERS *for* CHRISTIANS

# 84
## TRACKS

Tracks from wildlife are never straight. They meander in uncertain ways even in open terrain where there are no obstacles. Animals like foxes tread carefully over the exact same route. It's as if they sense a previous animal's footsteps. Humans, on the other hand, can walk straight through a field without wandering. Our steps are intentional and as direct as our motives are. Unlike animals we struggle with knowledge of our natural surroundings and with subtleties such as distress points, contextual and location cues. It's because we have choice we've no idea what it's like *not* to be able to choose. Animals are reactive and it shows in their tracks while our tracks reveal who we are.

*Lord, we pray that the tracks we leave behind have meaning for those who follow on.*

*Amen*

EVERYDAY FAITH

## 85
# BURDEN

Birthdays are easier to remember than deaths. With birthdays the person is still alive, although we can also bear to remember someone's birthday after they've died. But the day someone died or even the funeral date are not things we normally think of. In fact it's an emotional burden. There's one exception though. JESUS. HE'S the one person who we think of more on the day HE died, than on the day HE was born. And so it should be, because his death is the most important event for Christians. It's the day the burden we'd become to GOD, was lifted.

*Thank you Lord, for your mercy in lifting the burden we'd become; and sparing those with enough faith in your resurrection and forgiveness.*

*Amen*

LETTERS *for* CHRISTIANS

## 86
## ASSURED

As the psalmists says, in the morning we proclaim GOD's love and at night, HIS faithfulness. Grounding our faith in this way brings us certainty in the morning and peace at night. It's at the start of the day that we love HIS sureness and at the end of the day that we're assured in HIS love. And we can be sure that, whatever happens in between, HIS forgiveness reigns supreme.

*Thank you Lord, because we can count on your love and faithfulness.*

*Amen*

EVERYDAY FAITH

## 87
## SET FREE

The things we take for granted, how incredible this creation is;
and through it all we know so little, we seem so insignificant.

Yet even in the little we can conceive we're thrilled by GOD's deeds;
and at what his hands have done, we all shall concede.

How indescribable will be our joy when set free we see our LORD;
and in HIS kingdom we'll see ourselves, as all of us should be.

*Praise your name Lord, for it's not over until you say it is.*

*Amen*

LETTERS *for* CHRISTIANS

## 88
## EVERY DAY

*The righteous ... will still bear fruit in old age, they will stay fresh and green.* In this life it's hard to imagine starting again at an old age but the bare piece of land in front of us is testimony that we're everyday disciples doing everyday things. The wells of Abraham and Isaac produced life-giving water—like the well that we most hold on to today, which is our faith in you Lord.

**Help us Lord, to bear fruit in our old age so that all may see who we belong to— the King of all kings and Lord of lords.**

*Amen*

EVERYDAY FAITH

## 89
## ISOLATED

For those of us who've lived on an isolated property like a farm or some conservation area, the sight of a big truck approaching from a distance is exciting. We can normally tell from the sound what kind of delivery it is, such as diesel, coal, or feed for the livestock. The same truck in a city has no effect on us but out here, we're thrilled by the meaning. The sight of a removals truck is far less exciting if it's coming for us. So too a funeral hearse, coming for someone close. But when we're isolated the sound of just about anything can be exciting. Many of GOD's most faithful servants have lived in isolated conditions. It seems to be perfect for listening to THE LORD. So good, that when those trucks arrive we're ready to share in everything we've learnt out there. It's true also of our cities where many are living in a wilderness—completely isolated.

*Lord, may we be thankful for those you send to us, whether we're isolated on a farm or in a big city.*

*Amen*

LETTERS *for* CHRISTIANS

# 90
# REFLECTION

It's good that we reflect often about what it is we're trying to do, what role we think we should play, what church we should go to, who we should be friends with, where we should live, what job is right for us, how much money we should be saving, and so on. The list is endless when we concern ourselves with what we think we should be doing. It's not wrong, in fact, it's wise that we should think and plan ahead. But there's one thing we often forget which is that reflection isn't just analysing or planning—the most important thing is to listen.

*Lord, may we listen to what you have to say so that we know how to prioritise the things that need doing.*

*Amen*

EVERYDAY FAITH

## 91

**DEAR LORD**

As the psalmist says: *You are upright; our Rock, and there is no wickedness in You.* Our faith tells us so. As we go through the trials and tribulations that this world brings to our doorstep, grant us through your mercy, the peace that only you can provide. If we're writing a letter to You now Lord, then we've made it this far. Sometimes we wonder what the reason is for still being here but we know it's not the right question to ask. What we should be thinking to ourselves is what's left to do because there's only one reason we're still here and that's because there's still work for us to do. And you want us to do it. How special we may feel if, in your merciful love, we're able to complete the race you've set us to run.

What a blessing our walk of faith is because we don't need to be the fastest, strongest, most popular, cleverest, biggest, or richest. We only need to love you.

*Amen*

LETTERS *for* CHRISTIANS

# PSALM 92

**A psalm. A song. For the Sabbath day.**

1. It is good to praise the Lord
   and make music to your name, O Most High,
2. proclaiming your love in the morning
   and your faithfulness at night,
3. to the music of the ten-stringed lyre
   and the melody of the harp.

4. For you make me glad by your deeds, Lord;
   I sing for joy at what your hands have done.
5. How great are your works, Lord,
   how profound your thoughts!
6. Senseless people do not know,
   fools do not understand,
7. that though the wicked spring up like grass
   and all evildoers flourish,
   they will be destroyed forever.

8 But you, Lord, are forever exalted.
9 For surely your enemies, Lord,
   surely your enemies will perish;
   all evildoers will be scattered.
10 You have exalted my horn like that of a wild ox;
   fine oils have been poured on me.
11 My eyes have seen the defeat of my adversaries;
   my ears have heard the rout of my wicked foes.

12 The righteous will flourish like a palm tree,
   they will grow like a cedar of Lebanon;
13 planted in the house of the Lord,
   they will flourish in the courts of our God.
14 They will still bear fruit in old age,
   they will stay fresh and green,
15 proclaiming, "The Lord is upright;
   he is my Rock, and there is no wickedness in him." (NIV)

*Amen*

www.ingramcontent.com/pod-product-compliance
Lightning Source LLC
Chambersburg PA
CBHW041504010526
44118CB00001B/9